Thinking Critically:
The Death Penalty

Other titles in the *Thinking Critically* series include:

Thinking Critically:
The Death Penalty

Stephanie Watson

ReferencePoint
Press®

San Diego, CA

ACKNOWLEDGMENT
*The editor wishes to thank Lauri Scherer
for her assistance with this book.*

For more information, contact:
ReferencePoint Press, Inc.
PO Box 27779
San Diego, CA 92198
www.ReferencePointPress.com

Picture Credits:
Charts and graphs by Maury Aaseng

LIBRARY OF CONGRESS CATALOGING-IN-PUBLICATION DATA

Name: Watson, Stephanie, author.
Title: Thinking Critically: The Death Penalty/by Stephanie Watson.
Description: San Diego, CA: ReferencePoint Press, Inc., 2018. | Series: Thinking Critically series | Includes bibliographical references and index. | Audience: Grades 9 to 12.
Identifiers: ISBN 9781682822661 (eBook) | ISBN 9781682822654 (hardback)

Contents

Foreword

"Literacy is the most basic currency of the knowledge economy we're living in today." Barack Obama (at the time a senator from Illinois) spoke these words during a 2005 speech before the American Library Association. One question raised by this statement is: What does it mean to be a literate person in the twenty-first century?

E.D. Hirsch Jr., author of *Cultural Literacy: What Every American Needs to Know*, answers the question this way: "To be culturally literate is to possess the basic information needed to thrive in the modern world. The breadth of the information is great, extending over the major domains of human activity from sports to science."

But literacy in the twenty-first century goes beyond the accumulation of knowledge gained through study and experience and expanded over time. Now more than ever literacy requires the ability to sift through and evaluate vast amounts of information and, as the authors of the Common Core State Standards state, to "demonstrate the cogent reasoning and use of evidence that is essential to both private deliberation and responsible citizenship in a democratic republic."

The *Thinking Critically* series challenges students to become discerning readers, to think independently, and to engage and develop their skills as critical thinkers. Through a narrative-driven, pro/con format, the series introduces students to the complex issues that dominate public discourse—topics such as gun control and violence, social networking, and medical marijuana. Each chapter revolves around a single, pointed question such as Can Stronger Gun Control Measures Prevent Mass Shootings?, or Does Social Networking Benefit Society?, or Should Medical Marijuana Be Legalized? This inquiry-based approach introduces student researchers to core issues and concerns on a given topic. Each chapter includes one part that argues the affirmative and one part that argues the negative—all written by a single author. With the single-author format the predominant arguments for and against an issue can be synthesized into clear, accessible discussions supported by details and evidence including relevant facts, direct quotes, current examples, and statistical illustrations. All volumes include focus questions to guide students as they read each pro/con discussion, a list of key facts, and an annotated list of related organizations and websites for conducting further research.

The authors of the Common Core State Standards have set out the particular qualities that a literate person in the twenty-first century must have. These include the ability to think independently, establish a base of knowledge across a wide range of subjects, engage in open-minded but discerning reading and listening, know how to use and evaluate evidence, and appreciate and understand diverse perspectives. The new *Thinking Critically* series supports these goals by providing a solid introduction to the study of pro/con issues.

The Death Penalty

On the evening of June 17, 2015, a group of parishioners gathered for a Bible study session in the basement of Emanuel African Methodist Episcopal Church in Charleston, South Carolina. Emanuel is a historically black church, but on that night, a young white man named Dylann Roof joined the group. He was welcomed in, and he sat quietly listening as those around him read a passage from the Gospel of Mark. After about an hour, Roof stood up, pulled out a gun, and methodically began to shoot the people around him. By the time he was finished, nine parishioners lay dead or dying. A pastor, a mother of three, a recent college graduate, and a grandmother were among the dead.

As the victims' families and the community at large mourned, it became clear that Roof was a white supremacist whose motive was to incite a race war. No one disagreed that this was a heinous crime. The question was, how to punish him? The State of South Carolina and US attorney general Loretta E. Lynch called for the death penalty. Prosecutors said Roof had "demonstrated a lack of remorse," and had caused "injury, harm and loss to the individuals that he killed as well as to the family, friends, and co-workers of those individuals."[1]

Yet many survivors, victims' family members, and Justice Department officials called for prison time instead. Some felt that the death penalty was unethical or went against their Christian beliefs. Others feared that the years of protracted appeals and legal battles that might follow the verdict would only prolong their pain and suffering. Still others felt that executing Roof would let him off the hook in a sense, freeing him from being reminded of the pain and suffering he had caused. "I want that guy every morning when he wakes up, and every time he has an opportunity for quiet and solitude, to think of what Tywanza said to him: 'We mean you no harm. You don't have to do this,'"[2] said Charleston lawyer Andrew J. Savage III. (He was referring to twenty-six-year-old Tywanza Sanders, who died in the attack.)

Roof was ultimately sentenced to death. However, all of the issues raised during his trial illustrate the great debate that has surrounded the death penalty throughout much of America's history. Capital punishment—putting a convicted criminal to death—is the most serious of punishments, and is today reserved for only the most serious of crimes. Arguments over the death penalty touch on many issues, including human rights, racism, religious beliefs, the essence of justice, and the value placed on human life—that of both the victim and the perpetrator.

The Death Penalty Throughout History

The death penalty has existed in Western civilization for thousands of years. In ancient Egypt it was used to punish crimes such as assassinating a king, robbing a tomb, and engaging in corruption. The Babylonian Code of Hammurabi, written on clay tablets in 1760 BCE, included laws supporting capital punishment for twenty-five crimes—among them committing adultery and helping a slave escape.

The Bible seems to send mixed messages about death as punishment. The Old Testament introduced the idea of an "eye for an eye." God told Noah, "Whoever sheds the blood of man, by man shall his blood be shed; for God made man in his own image."[3] Yet the New Testament appears to urge forgiveness rather than severe punishment.

Britain, like much of the rest of Europe, allowed for capital punishment in its criminal justice system. The American colonies modeled their legal system on Britain's criminal codes, which allowed for the death penalty for those found guilty of crimes such as treason, rape, and murder. The first known execution in the American colonies was in 1608, when George Kendall of Virginia was hanged for spying for the Spanish.

Capital punishment was legal in both Europe and early America, but many people found the idea morally repugnant. This rejection of the

States With and Without the Death Penalty, 2017

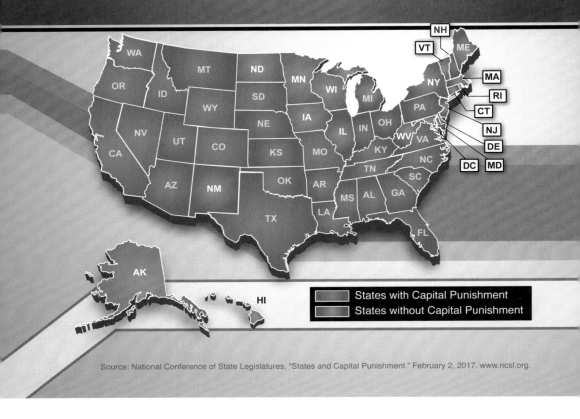

Source: National Conference of State Legislatures, "States and Capital Punishment." February 2, 2017. www.ncsl.org.

death penalty led to an abolition movement on both sides of the Atlantic Ocean during the 1700s. The Eighth Amendment of the US Bill of Rights prohibited "cruel and unusual punishment," but provides no examples of what constitutes such a punishment. And even though capital punishment remained legal, many people were still uncomfortable using the death penalty, even for crimes such as murder. In 1797 American founding father Benjamin Rush wrote, "The punishment of murder by death is contrary to reason, and to the order and happiness of society."[4]

In 1845 the first national group dedicated to ending this form of punishment—the American Society for the Abolition of Capital Punishment—was founded in the United States. A year later, Michigan became the first state to abolish the death penalty for all crimes but treason. Rhode Island was the first state to do away with the death penalty entirely, in 1852.

Changing Public Opinion

Throughout the nineteenth and twentieth centuries, a number of states wavered between allowing and abolishing the death penalty. Public opinion about the practice also swung back and forth over the years.

One development that led to more acceptance of the death penalty was improvements in execution technology. Slow, barbaric methods like burning alive or crucifixion were replaced by seemingly quicker and more humane methods, such as hanging and the firing squad. In 1792 French physician Joseph-Ignace Guillotin devised a machine in which a heavy blade was dropped between two posts onto the accused's neck. The idea was to behead the person in an instant, preventing pain and suffering. (Unfortunately, often the guillotine's blade did not fall as intended, and the victim was left gravely injured and in great pain.)

In 1890, with the help of inventor Thomas Edison, the electric chair was introduced. A shock of up to two thousand volts was meant to be a more rapid, and therefore more humane, mode of death—yet it was anything but humane. Convicted murderer William Kemmler of Buffalo, New York, was the first person to die by this method. After the first jolt, Kemmler remained alive. Blood began to seep from his face, and the smell of burning skin permeated the death chamber. "The stench was unbearable,"[5] one witness observed.

Finally, lethal injection was introduced in 1982. The injection contains a cocktail of medicines that put the convicted person to sleep before causing death. Today, lethal injection is the primary method of execution in the United States.

Two Capital Cases

A pivotal moment in the death penalty debate came in 1972, with the *Furman v. Georgia* case. During a burglary attempt, William Furman accidentally killed a member of the family he was trying to rob. Despite the accidental nature of the crime, Furman was convicted and sentenced to death. The US Supreme Court ruled five to four that the death penalty was arbitrary and unconstitutional as administered. It put a de facto moratorium on executions—a rule that essentially paused all future executions. Anyone who was on death row at the time was resentenced to serve a prison term.

But just four years later, following a rise in violent crimes, public opinion again shifted. The Supreme Court reversed its 1972 decision during the 1976 case *Gregg v. Georgia*. Troy Gregg had been found guilty of a double murder and sentenced to death in Georgia. The Supreme Court reinstated the death penalty, ruling that Georgia's system for applying it was "judicious" and "careful."[6]

The court adopted a new sentencing approach to help ensure that death penalty cases were handled fairly. In the first stage, the guilty defendant was convicted of the crime. In the second, sentencing stage, the jury could impose the death sentence only if it found an "aggravating circumstance"—for example, if the crime was truly heinous, or the perpetrator showed a lack of remorse. In addition the jury could instead impose a life sentence if it found "mitigating evidence"—for example, information that the accused had had a difficult life or had been abused as a child. Capital punishment law has been refined a few times since then. For example, children and the mentally disabled can no longer be executed.

The Death Penalty Today

Public support for the death penalty has continued to rise and fall over the years. In the 1980s and early 1990s, when Americans were concerned about rising crime rates, support was as high as 80 percent. Yet by the 2000s, support hovered at around 60 percent, the decline in support fueled in part by questions about false accusations. With the advent of DNA testing, experts have sometimes determined that the person accused of the crime did not actually commit it.

As of 2017, thirty-one states—more than half—still allowed the death penalty. Other countries were more steadfast in their determination to abolish the death penalty. In November 2007 the United Nations

General Assembly adopted a resolution calling for a worldwide moratorium on the death penalty, and in 2014 then UN secretary-general Ban Ki-moon declared, "The death penalty has no place in the 21st century."[7] In 2014 Pope Francis also called for a universal abolition of the practice. As many other nations around the world set aside the death penalty, the practice of capital punishment—and the controversies surrounding it—continues in the United States.

Chapter One

Does the Death Penalty Deter Crime?

The Death Penalty Deters Crime

- Research shows that each execution prevents other murders from taking place—as few as 2.5 and as many as 18.
- The death penalty makes people fear the consequences of committing murder; most people are afraid of death, so they will avoid it by any possible means.
- The faster the death penalty is meted out, the more of a deterrent it becomes.
- Executing a murderer prevents him or her from ever killing again.

The Debate at a Glance

The Death Penalty Does Not Deter Crime

- Research does not support the idea that capital punishment deters crime; studies that suggest that it does have used flawed research methods.
- Murder rates tend to be lower in places without the death penalty and higher in places with it, which indicates it has no deterrent effect.
- Deterrence does not apply to certain types of crime—such as crimes of passion or terrorism, or those committed by psychopaths.
- Executing murderers to incapacitate them is ineffective; it is impossible to predict who will commit multiple crimes, and the system cannot execute every murderer.

The Death Penalty Deters Crime

"Allowing defendants in child murder cases to be eligible for the death penalty was associated with an almost 20 percent reduction in rates of these crimes. In short, capital punishment does, in fact, save lives."

—David B. Muhlhausen, research fellow for the Heritage Foundation

David B. Muhlhausen, "How the Death Penalty Saves Lives," *U.S. News & World Report*, September 29, 2014. www.usnews.com.

Consider these questions as you read:

1. Which piece of evidence did you think best supported the argument that the death penalty deters crime? What did you find compelling about it?
2. How might executing murderers more quickly make the death penalty more of a deterrent?
3. Based on what you read about the idea of deterrence, would you support or oppose the death penalty? Explain your reasoning.

Editor's note: The discussion that follows presents common arguments made in support of this perspective, reinforced by facts, quotes, and examples taken from various sources.

The death penalty is the ultimate punishment, one even that murderers fear. In fact, the idea that the death penalty deters—which means discourages or prevents—people from committing crimes in the first place is one of the death penalty's main assets. It has been repeatedly proved that people are less likely to commit murder if they fear they will be put to death in return. In this way the mere existence of the death penalty helps save lives.

Executions Discourage Crime

Multiple studies have found evidence of the death penalty's deterrent effect. For example, in a 2003 study by Emory University, researchers looked at data from more than three thousand state counties that was collected between 1977 and 1996. They found that on average each execution caused murder rates to drop, resulting in 18 fewer murders per county. In another study that looked at data from all fifty states during a similar time frame, economist Paul Zimmerman found that each state execution detered about 14 murders each year. A different group of researchers led by Kenneth Land of Duke University found that from 1994 to 2005, each execution that took place in Texas was associated with 2.5 fewer murders.

Just knowing they could be eligible for execution makes at least some criminals think twice about whether they want to go ahead with their crime. This was borne out by a 2009 study in which researchers looked at what happened when defendants in child murder cases suddenly became eligible to receive the death penalty if they were found guilty. Researchers found that when states adopted these harsher sentencing laws, the prevalence of these crimes dropped by nearly 20 percent. This is why people like David Muhlhausen, a research fellow for the Heritage Foundation, regard the death penalty as "morally just." It is just, he says, because "it may just save the lives of several innocents."[8]

Conversely, suspending capital punishment corresponds with a rise in murders. University of Illinois professors Dale Cloninger and Roberto Marchesini found this to be true when they looked at homicides committed in Texas in the 1900s. In 1996 Texas put a one-year moratorium (or pause) on all executions; the moratorium ended in 1997. After reviewing data, the researchers found that the one-year suspension was associated with about 220 additional murders in the state.

Rewards and Penalties

Setting statistics aside, however, it just makes sense that the death penalty would present a logical deterrent. People who commit murder are like everyone else—they consider their own self-interests when making

Voters Continue to Support Death Penalty

Voters in three states yet again showed strong support for the death penalty in 2016. Death penalty proponents often cite the deterrence effect as one reason for their continued support. In Nebraska, 61.2 percent voted in favor of a referendum repealing an earlier decision to do away with the state's death penalty law. In Oklahoma, 66.4 percent agreed that the death penalty is not cruel or unusual and thus should be retained. Even in California, considered one of the most liberal states, 53.6 percent said no to a repeal of that state's death penalty law.

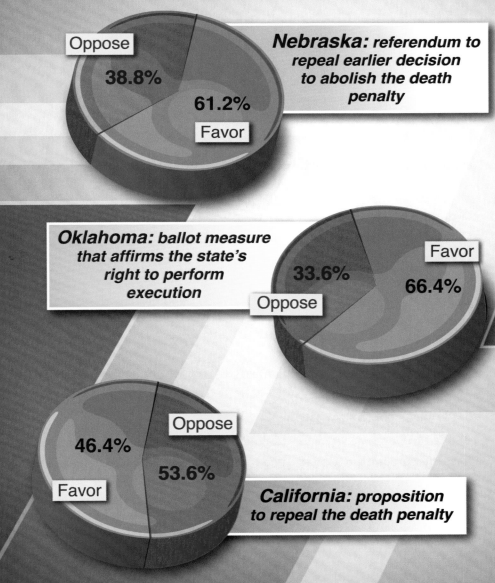

Oppose 38.8%

Favor 61.2%

Nebraska: *referendum to repeal earlier decision to abolish the death penalty*

Oklahoma: *ballot measure that affirms the state's right to perform execution*

33.6% Oppose

Favor 66.4%

46.4% Favor

Oppose 53.6%

California: *proposition to repeal the death penalty*

Source: Aliyah Frumin, "Election 2016: Nebraska, Oklahoma vote in Favor of Death Penalty," NBC News, November 9, 2016. www.nbcnews.com.

decisions. Their actions are based on perceived rewards and consequences. If they feel the negative consequences of their crime will exceed the reward, they are less likely to commit it.

Think about it: The reason most people don't walk into a jewelry store and simply take a necklace they admire is that they fear going to jail. Similarly, when people debate whether to take a life, they think about the possibility that they might be executed. It's simply part of human nature to consider consequences.

> "I'll shoot everyone in the bank. The Supreme Court will let me get away with this. There's no death penalty."[9]
>
> —John Wojtowicz, a bank robber

This proved true for John Wojtowicz, who robbed a Brooklyn, New York, bank in the early 1970s. The robbery occurred after the Supreme Court decided to halt the death penalty in the the landmark case *Furman v. Georgia*. Wojtowicz reportedly threatened to kill eight hostages, saying, "I'll shoot everyone in the bank. The Supreme Court will let me get away with this. There's no death penalty. . . . I can shoot everyone here, then throw my gun down and walk out, and they can't put me in the electric chair."[9]

Even the most hardened murderers are inherently afraid of death because of its finality. "I fear death more than imprisonment because it alone takes from me all future possibility,"[10] philosopher Louis P. Pojman once said. This is why many prisoners spend decades appealing their death sentences—because they, like all people, want to live as long as possible.

To Deter, Punishment Must Be Swift

Of course, to be an effective deterrent, the death penalty must be used in a timely way. Imagine that an innocent person is murdered, but the perpetrator is not executed for years and years. Then, decades after the crime, the perpetrator is finally put to death. Those who sought justice for the victim would have long since moved on with their lives, and many would have even died themselves. In these circumstances, would the killer's punishment still have meaning? Would other potential criminals even notice that the killer had been executed?

Now consider that if every time an innocent person was killed, the perpetrator was immediately executed. Other would-be murderers would witness this severe punishment repeated over and over again. Knowing they would be put to death soon after they killed would very likely dissuade them from carrying out any similar plans. This is the argument of Pojman and many others who say that the faster and more publicly punishment is meted out, the more effective a deterrent it becomes.

The death penalty can only be an effective deterrent if it is used often, consistently, and quickly. However, prisoners today remain on death row for extended periods of time, filing appeal after appeal to delay their ultimate punishment. The average time that elapses between sentencing and execution is more than fifteen years, according to the US Department of Justice. If killers think it will be decades before they will be executed, they will not view the death penalty as a serious deterrent.

A Dead Murderer Cannot Kill Again

Even if execution is delayed, however, the death penalty deters murderers because it stops convicted killers from ever committing another murder. Someone who has killed once is likely to do so again, but if that person is dead, he or she can never kill again. One case that proves this logic true comes from 1983, when eighteen-year-old Corey Robert Barton was convicted of beating and stabbing Shari-Ann Merton to death. Barton served just eight years in prison before the state of Connecticut released him for good behavior in 1992. "We kept telling everybody, 'He will kill again,'"[11] said Gary Merton, Shari-Ann's father. Then, in 1998, Barton did just that. He murdered his ex-girlfriend, Sally Harris, in North Carolina. Had Barton been executed for his first crime, Harris's life would have been spared.

> "I fear death more than imprisonment because it alone takes from me all future possibility."[10]
>
> —Louis P. Pojman, philosopher

Sentencing murderers to life in prison does not prevent them from causing further harm. For one thing, the criminal justice system is imperfect. Prisoners can be released early for good behavior, for example.

Even those who remain in prison for the rest of their lives can kill people around them—guards or other prisoners. Bennie Demps committed two murders in 1971 and was sentenced to death. However, he was not executed because the Supreme Court ruled the death penalty unconstitutional in 1972. In September 1976 Demps was involved in the murder of a fellow prisoner at Florida State Prison. If Demps had been executed for his first crime, he never would have had the chance to repeat it.

Murderers Cannot Be Rehabilitated

Those who oppose the death penalty suggest that murderers can be rehabilitated, but psychologists say that the most disturbed psychopaths—the people most likely to kill—can never be reformed. Research finds that these killers have abnormalities in parts of their brain that prevent them from feeling the empathy and guilt that keep others from committing murder. The only course of action to stop these murderers is to put them to death. Robert S. Henry, a retired capital case coordinator with the California attorney general's office, reminds us that having the death penalty is for our own protection. "The minute you remove any possible punishment for killing, you are removing a deterrent for some potential killer," says Henry. "It's not about [the criminals'] lives; it is about protecting your own life from those to whom the death penalty is a deterrent."[12]

The Death Penalty Does Not Deter Crime

"The question of whether executions discourage criminals from violent acts is not up to the conscience to decide. Despite extensive research on the question, criminologists have been unable to assemble a strong case that capital punishment deters crime."

—Max Ehrenfreund, reporter for the *Washington Post*

Max Ehrenfreund, "There's Still No Evidence That Executions Deter Criminals," *Washington Post,* April 30, 2014. www.washingtonpost.com.

Consider these questions as you read:

1. Both pro and con arguments for the deterrence effect of the death penalty use statistical research to support their position. How do you account for this? Which statistics can be trusted, in your opinion?
2. Opponents of the death penalty argue that it might actually lead to an increase in murders. Evaluate this argument. Is it sound? Why or why not?
3. What kinds of criminals might be unaffected by the threat of receiving the death penalty? Explain why.

Editor's note: The discussion that follows presents common arguments made in support of this perspective, reinforced by facts, quotes, and examples taken from various sources.

Death penalty supporters often argue that executing murderers discourages other would-be criminals from committing crimes. However, this is a deeply flawed argument; when closely examined it is revealed to be illogical, poorly supported, and not borne out by research. In actuality, the death penalty has no such deterrent effect, which is among the many reasons it should be abolished.

Flawed Studies

Studies that claim capital punishment reduces murders have been inconsistent, inconclusive, and otherwise flawed. In fact, many legal scholars have questioned the methods used in these studies, suggesting the science behind them was dubious. For example, Jeffrey Fagan, a professor at Columbia Law School, found that most such studies do not take into account the existence of life sentences or high incarceration rates, which are other factors that may lower murder rates. In other words, the authors of the flawed studies claim that the death penalty led to fewer murders when in fact the lower murder rate might have been due to these other factors. Furthermore, studies that do show a connection between the death penalty and deterrence are poorly designed, according to Stanford University law professor John Donohue. "All of these studies collapse after errors in coding, measuring statistical significance, or in establishing causal relationships are corrected," he says. "There is not the slightest credible statistical evidence that capital punishment reduces the rate of homicide."[13]

> "There is not the slightest credible statistical evidence that capital punishment reduces the rate of homicide."[13]
>
> —John Donohue, Stanford University law professor

On the other hand, numerous studies have shown no connection between the death penalty and deterrence. Perhaps most convincing of these was an exhaustive 2012 survey undertaken by a panel from the National Academy of Sciences. After reviewing all the available research on the subject, it found no evidence that the death penalty is a deterrent. In fact, the authors of the survey found so little to indicate a connection that they recommended "the issue of deterrence should be removed from any discussion of the death penalty given this lack of credible evidence."[14]

No Death Penalty, Fewer Murders

Evidence of a deterrent effect becomes even weaker when one compares actual homicide numbers to the existence of state death penalty laws. Even as many states have abolished capital punishment, the rate of violent crime has dropped. The same is true in states that retain the practice but execute fewer and fewer people. Evidence actually shows that parts of the country without a death penalty statute have fewer murders than ones with capital punishment. In fact, the South, which executes a greater number of people, has the higher murder rate. Meanwhile, the North, which executes fewer people, has the lower rate. This could indicate that the presence of the death penalty tends to encourage murder, rather than deter it. In fact, rather than deterring crime, it is more likely that capital punishment actually has a "brutalization effect." The theory behind this idea suggests that when states execute criminals, it lowers the public's respect for life and desensitizes people to death. This can lead to an increase in murders.

This pattern is not just true in the United States; in countries and cities around the world, evidence suggests that the presence of a death penalty is linked to higher crime rates, while the absence of one is linked to lower crime rates. One example comes from Asia. Researchers compared murder rates in Hong Kong, which has not had the death penalty since 1993, with murder rates in Singapore, where convicted killers get the death penalty (typically in less than two years of being convicted). The researchers found no significant difference in murder rates between the two places, leading them to conclude that the death penalty does not have a deterrent effect. "We're very hard pressed to find really strong evidence of deterrence,"[15] says Fagan, who was one of the study's coauthors.

There Are No Deterrents to Some Crimes

One reason the death penalty is not effective is the fact that it is not likely to deter several types of criminals. One type are criminals who are mentally ill and/or have no sense of right and wrong, and thus don't base their decisions on consequences. Psychologists have found that the most disturbed psychopaths—the people most likely to kill—have abnormalities in parts of their brain that prevent them from feeling emotions like empathy and guilt. These are among the emotions that prevent people from committing crime, especially murder. It stands to reason, then, that psychopaths would not be disturbed by the potential consequences that

Highest Murder Rates Occur in Death Penalty States

If the death penalty deters crime, then it follows that crime should be lower in states that have the death penalty. But this is not the case where murder is concerned. According to figures from 2015, which are the latest statistics available, murder rates in death penalty states are actually higher than in states that do not have the death penalty. In fact, studies show that states without the death penalty have had consistently lower murder rates dating back to the 1990s.

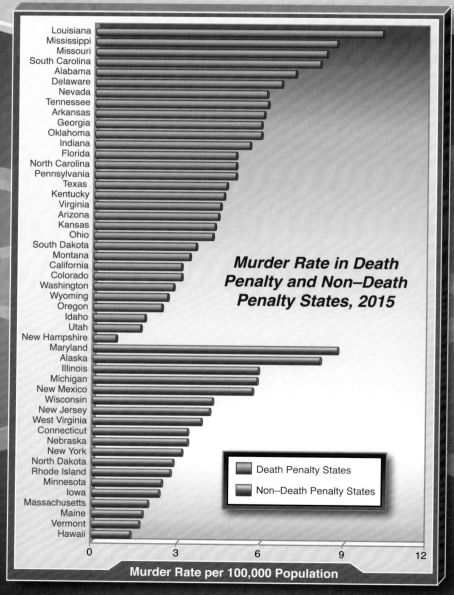

Murder Rate in Death Penalty and Non–Death Penalty States, 2015

Death Penalty States
Non–Death Penalty States

Murder Rate per 100,000 Population

Source: Death Penalty Information Center, "Deterrence: States Without the Death Penalty Have Had Consistently Lower Murder Rates," 2017. https://deathpenaltyinfo.org.

would cause others to stop cold in their tracks. As Donohue puts it, "The likelihood is incredibly remote that some small chance of execution many years after committing a crime will influence the behavior of a sociopathic deviant who would otherwise be willing to kill if his only penalty were life imprisonment."[16]

The death penalty would also not deter anyone who committed a crime in the heat of the moment—a so-called crime of passion. Such crimes are not planned in advance, and the killers had no intention of killing prior to finding themselves in the act of doing so. In such cases, the effect of capital punishment seems irrelevant. Since their crimes are not premeditated, these killers are not thinking about whether they will take the risk of being executed. No punishment, then, could alter the course such people embark upon.

Similar logic can be applied to those who are involved in organized criminal enterprises such as terrorist groups. There are people who kill in the name of an ideal—such as to defend a territory or a religious belief or to further some other cause. Such criminals have proved they are willing to kill themselves as part

> "Those who plant bombs apparently are not afraid of death."[17]
>
> —Florence Bellivier, former president of the World Coalition Against the Death Penalty, and Dimitris Christopoulos, president of the human rights organization FIDH

of their crimes, so surely the threat of execution would not deter them. "Those who plant bombs apparently are not afraid of death," note Florence Bellivier, former president of the World Coalition Against the Death Penalty, and Dimitris Christopoulos, president of the human rights organization FIDH. Moreover, executing terrorists would be counterproductive, as doing so would make them martyrs for their cause and even serve to promote it. "To top it off, capital punishment can be used by these same terrorists to convince their troops that reprisal is justified, and thus feed into the cycle of violence,"[17] say Bellivier and Christopoulos.

Who Knows Who Is Likely to Kill Again?

That the death penalty would prevent someone from ever killing again is also untrue. This idea is based on the concept of recidivism—that a person who has committed one crime will go on to commit another one. It is certainly true that if a person is executed for committing murder, that person cannot go on to commit another crime. But how many murderers actually would have committed another crime if they had not been put to death? It is impossible to predict which murderers have the potential to commit another serious crime, and which ones can be rehabilitated or made to feel remorse for their crime. The truth is, not all murderers do kill again.

Getting Caught Is the Real Deterrent

While criminals are clearly not influenced by how they might be punished, nearly all of them do care about not getting caught—this is evidenced by the lengths to which they go to avoid doing so. This reveals that the real deterrent to murder is not severe punishment—it is getting caught. Indeed, most criminals are primarily concerned with not getting captured for a crime; they don't necessarily focus on what will happen after that. "It's the certainty of apprehension that's been demonstrated consistently to be an effective deterrent," says Daniel Nagin, a professor of public policy at Carnegie Mellon University, "not the severity of the ensuing consequences."[18]

The death penalty, then, does nothing to deter crime. Most criminals do not stop to consider or even care about the severity of the punishment they will receive for committing a crime. Studies claiming that they do are deeply flawed. In the end, putting a killer to death does nothing to lower crime rates or keep people safe.

Chapter Two

Is the Death Penalty Fairly Imposed?

The Death Penalty Is Fairly Imposed

- The Supreme Court has refined the death penalty over the years to make it more fair and consistent. Death penalty cases are carefully and thoroughly litigated, first in state courts and then in federal court.
- Anyone who is sentenced to death has numerous chances to appeal the sentence and prove his or her innocence.
- DNA evidence is helping to prevent innocent people from being wrongfully executed.
- Racial discrimination is far less of a problem today than it was in the past, in part because people can now challenge their sentence if they believe it was based on racial bias.

The Debate at a Glance

The Death Penalty Is Not Fairly Imposed

- The death penalty is unfairly biased against minorities, poor people, and those who live in states that impose it.
- Minorities make up a disproportionate number of inmates on death row, while juries are overwhelmingly white.
- Use of the death penalty is unfair because it is unevenly applied from state to state.
- Innocent people have ended up on death row and have likely been executed.

The Death Penalty Is Fairly Imposed

"We should not hesitate to impose the death penalty when DNA testing creates such a high probability of guilt beyond any reasonable doubt."

—Lee Atkinson, criminal defense attorney

Lee Atkinson, "DNA Evidence, Testing Make Death Penalty More Credible," *Orlando Sentinel,* October 30, 2012. http://articles.orlandosentinel.com.

Consider these questions as you read:

1. Do you think the Supreme Court's refinements to the death penalty over the years have made it more fair? Why or why not?
2. In your opinion, are innocent people likely to be executed? Why or why not?
3. Do you think racism continues to be a problem in the application of the death penalty? Why or why not?

Editor's note: The discussion that follows presents common arguments made in support of this perspective, reinforced by facts, quotes, and examples taken from various sources.

Death penalty cases are never considered lightly. The Supreme Court has repeatedly refined the death penalty to make sure it is fairly imposed. Given the strong laws regarding the death penalty's use and modern technology's help in ensuring that people who get the death penalty are guilty, Americans can rest assured that the death penalty is justly applied and reserved for the most deserving of cases.

An Exhaustive and Lengthy Process

One reason to trust that the death penalty is applied fairly is the amount of scrutiny each death penalty case gets. Today, death penalty cases must

Americans Say the Death Penalty Is Applied Fairly

Critics often complain that the death penalty is not applied fairly. One frequent criticism, for instance, is that blacks are more likely to receive the death penalty than whites. Despite this and other criticisms, half of Americans polled in 2016 say they believe the death penalty is applied fairly. Similar polls show that more Americans have consistently held this view dating back to at least 2000.

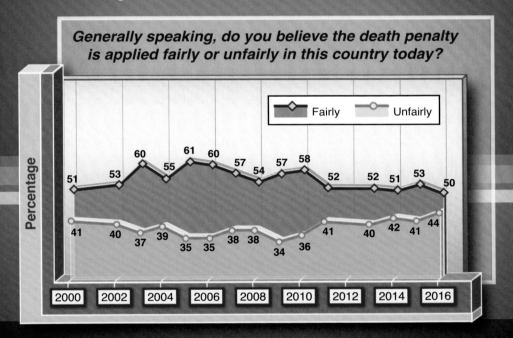

Generally speaking, do you believe the death penalty is applied fairly or unfairly in this country today?

Fairly — Unfairly

Percentage

Fairly: 51, 53, 60, 55, 61, 60, 57, 54, 57, 58, 52, 52, 51, 53, 50

Unfairly: 41, 40, 37, 39, 35, 35, 38, 38, 34, 36, 41, 40, 42, 41, 44

2000 2002 2004 2006 2008 2010 2012 2014 2016

Source: Gallup, "U.S. Death Penalty Support at 60%," October 25, 2016. www.gallup.com.

go through not one, but several challenging phases. First, the prosecutor must decide whether the crime was serious enough to justify the death penalty. In making this decision, the prosecutor must consider whether the defendant killed the victim intentionally, whether the murder was premeditated (planned), and if it occurred while the killer was committing another crime, like burglary or rape. If the crime meets any of these criteria, the prosecutor may seek the death penalty.

Then the case goes to trial, which has two phases. In the first phase, the jury decides whether the defendant is innocent or guilty. If the defendant is found guilty, during the second phase, the jury decides the penalty. To impose the death penalty, the jury has to find aggravating factors. These include, for example, the murderer being accused of killing several people, having a serious prior criminal record, showing no remorse, or committing the murder alongside another serious crime like rape. The jury must also consider mitigating factors that might lighten blame. These might include the murderer having a history of mental illness, experiencing an abusive childhood, or being under the influence of alcohol or drugs.

Once convicted and sentenced to death, the defendant can appeal his or her sentence to the highest state court. The court has the opportunity to reverse the decision if it feels the lower court made mistakes or if it concludes that the first trial was unfair. Defendants can also petition the Supreme Court if they feel their federal constitutional rights were violated.

If the Supreme Court denies this request, the defendant can still ask for further review through the state's post-conviction remedy procedure. He or she must raise claims that were not in the court records from the original trial—for example, the defendant might claim that an important defense witness was never called to the stand. The final step is called habeas corpus, and it challenges the legality of the sentence at the federal level. If the defendant is successful, he or she may get a retrial, or convince a judge to overturn the conviction or sentence.

All of these steps serve as a safeguard. They prevent the courts from misusing the death penalty or convicting the wrong person. The Bureau of Justice Statistics reports that as of 2017, inmates sentenced to death sat on death row for an average of 16.8 years before being executed. This lengthy amount of time serves to show that no one is executed hastily; the process is very thorough and exhaustive.

The Death Penalty Is Not Racist

Racism remains an issue in the United States, but its influence on death penalty cases has drastically diminished in the last few decades. In part, this is due to the 1972 Supreme Court case *Furman v. Georgia*. In that case, justices found that death sentences were often biased against black defendants, and so ruled that jurors are required to consider racial discrimination among a defendant's disadvantages when handing down a sentence. Those who are condemned to death are now allowed to appeal their sentence if they believe racial bias was at play in the decision.

This decision significantly changed the way the death penalty was applied in the decades going forward. By 2006 a study from the prominent research organization Rand found there is no evidence that race plays any role in federal prosecutors' decisions to seek the death penalty. Instead, it found that decisions are based on the type of crime committed.

Further showing the decline of racism in decisions about the death penalty is the racial makeup of those who are executed. From the 1930s to the 1960s, African Americans made up a disproportionally high percentage—54 percent—of people sent to death row. Since the late 1970s, however, whites have made up the majority of prisoners sentenced to death. According to the US Department of Justice, in 2013, 56 percent of prisoners on death row were white, while 42 percent were black. Even though African Americans commit more murders overall, today they are less likely to be executed than are whites.

It is true that African Americans are more likely to get the death penalty if they kill a white person than if they kill a black person, but there are reasons for this disparity. For one, black-on-black murders usually occur among people who know each other, and this type of crime typically does not qualify for a death penalty sentence. In contrast, when white people are the victims, the crime often involves an aggravating factor, such as rape or robbery, which does carry the death penalty.

Technology Reduces Wrongful Executions

Another development ensuring the fairness of the death penalty is the fact that it is easier than ever to prevent wrongful executions. Although an ongoing concern about the death penalty is that an innocent person could be mistakenly sentenced to death, the use of DNA evidence in recent years has reduced this possibility to almost zero.

DNA, or deoxyribonucleic acid, is the genetic material found in human cells. It contains unique instructions to make each person, and no two people's DNA (with the exception of identical twins) is exactly alike. DNA can be taken from saliva, semen, blood, skin, or hair samples left at a crime scene. It can be compared with samples taken from a suspect to help determine whether he or she committed the crime.

Thanks to the use of DNA evidence, executions of innocent people have become very rare. As late Supreme Court justice Antonin Scalia argued during the 2006 case *Kansas v. Marsh*, there is no evidence that even one person has been executed for a crime he or she did not commit. "If such an event had occurred in recent years, we would not have to hunt for it; the innocent's name would be shouted from the rooftops," Scalia wrote. Of DNA evidence, he added, "In every case of an executed defendant of which I am aware, that technology has *confirmed* guilt."[19]

> "In every case of an executed defendant of which I am aware, that technology has *confirmed* guilt."[19]
>
> —Former Supreme Court justice Antonin Scalia

An example of such DNA confirmation is the case of Ricky McGinn. He was sentenced to death for the 1993 rape and murder of his stepdaughter, Stephanie Flanary. McGinn professed his innocence and appealed his case. But when DNA tests were done, they clearly matched him to samples found on the victim. When he was executed on September 27, 2000, there was no doubt in anyone's mind that he was indeed guilty.

The Death Penalty Is Worth Its High Price

Clearly, wrongful executions have been reduced. But even if an innocent person were to be executed, it would be an acceptable cost. A strong criminal justice system that includes the death penalty protects millions from harm. "Like other human institutions, courts and juries are not perfect. One cannot have a system of criminal punishment without accepting the possibility that someone will be punished mistakenly," acknowledged Scalia in *Kansas v. Marsh*. "But with regard to the punishment of death in the current American system, that possibility has been reduced to an insignificant minimum."[20]

Wrongful execution is unlikely, as Scalia points out, but even if it does occur on rare occasions, it is still worth retaining the death penalty. "Many desirable social practices cannot avoid killing innocents by accident," writes Ernest van den Haag, a former professor of jurisprudence and public policy at Fordham University in New York. "For instance, ambulances save many lives, but also run over some pedestrians. We do not abolish ambulances, because they save more innocents than they kill."[21]

> "Many desirable social practices cannot avoid killing innocents by accident. For instance, ambulances save many lives, but also run over some pedestrians. We do not abolish ambulances, because they save more innocents than they kill."[21]
>
> —Ernest van den Haag, former professor of jurisprudence and public policy, Fordham University, New York

The death penalty definitely saves more innocents than it kills. With a strong process in place to ensure that death penalty sentences are imposed fairly, without racial bias, and accurately, with the help of DNA evidence, society can rest assured that the death penalty gives more than it takes away.

The Death Penalty Is Not Fairly Imposed

"The death penalty is imposed in the United States upon the poorest, most powerless, most marginalized people in the society. Virtually all of the people selected for execution are poor, about half are members of racial minorities, and the overwhelming majority were sentenced to death for crimes against white victims."

—Stephen B. Bright, president and senior counsel, Southern Center for Human Rights

Stephen B. Bright, "Imposition of the Death Penalty upon the Poor, Racial Minorities, the Intellectually Disabled, and the Mentally Ill," April 24, 2014. www.law.nyu.edu.

Consider these questions as you read:

1. How might having almost exclusively white prosecutors affect the outcome of death penalty trials involving minority defendants?
2. How might differences in death penalty laws from state to state contribute to inequity in the use of capital punishment?
3. Does DNA analysis solve the problem of innocent people being sentenced to death? Why or why not?

Editor's note: The discussion that follows presents common arguments made in support of this perspective, reinforced by facts, quotes, and examples taken from various sources.

Whether convicted killers receive the death penalty depends a great deal on their income, where they live, and the color of their skin. Because the death penalty is unfairly imposed upon poor people, minorities, and people who live in states that have capital punishment, it cannot be said to be justly or fairly applied.

Poor People Are Hit the Hardest

While those accused of murder have the right to defend themselves and even appeal the decision, doing so is monumentally expensive. Defense attorneys typically charge between $200 and $400 an hour, and such cases can last for months. Defendants who cannot afford to pay are assigned a court-appointed attorney, who might make just $65 an hour. Low pay and heavy caseloads force some public defenders to spend as little as one or two hours on cases that should take weeks to prepare—cases that will determine whether someone lives or dies.

Court-appointed lawyers are not only underpaid; in many cases, they are also unqualified. For example, when Gary Drinkard was sentenced to death in 1995 for robbery and murder, two court-appointed lawyers represented him. One lawyer specialized in collections and commercial work. The other dealt in foreclosures. Neither had any experience in criminal cases. Their inexperience caused Drinkard to be found guilty of a crime he did not commit. He spent nearly six years on death row before he was finally acquitted and released.

Some court-appointed attorneys fail to present any witnesses or evidence that would prove the defendant's innocence. Others are simply incompetent. Ronald Wayne Frye's attorney drank twelve shots of rum a day during the penalty phase of his trial, in which Frye was sentenced to execution. "As a result, the jury never heard mitigating evidence that likely would have saved Frye's life," writes the NC Coalition for Alternatives to the Death Penalty. "After the trial, some of the jurors said they would not have voted for a death sentence if they had known about the severe abuse Frye suffered as a child."[22] Similarly, three people were sentenced to death in Houston, Texas, during cases in which their court-appointed lawyers slept through parts of the proceedings.

The Death Penalty Is Racially Biased

In addition to being biased against the poor, the death penalty is also racially biased. According to the US Department of Justice, in 2013, 56 percent of all death row inmates were white and 42 percent were black. While these numbers might make it seem as if white people are more

Victim Race and Gender Unfairly Influence Executions

In Florida, which executed eighty-nine people between 1976 and 2014, statistics reveal that executions are heavily—and unfairly—influenced by the victim's race and gender. A 2016 study shows that a crime is much more likely to result in execution when the victim is a white female than when the victim is a black male or even a black female or white male. Although this study focuses on one state, it represents a much larger problem of fairness in how the death penalty is applied.

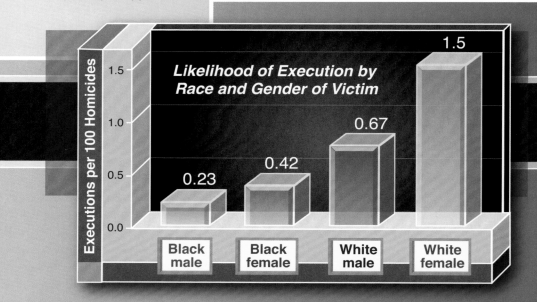

Source: Frank R. Baumgartner, "The Impact of Race, Gender, and Geography on Florida Executions," University of North Carolina, Chapel Hill, January 14, 2016. www.unc.edu.

likely to get sentenced to death, consider the relative size of each population. In 2013 whites made up about 77 percent of the US population. African Americans made up just 13 percent. Clearly, the death penalty is disproportionately applied to African Americans.

Meanwhile, the vast majority of prosecutors and attorneys are white, as are juries. In the town of Dothan, Alabama, one-third of the residents—and two-thirds of people who are arrested for crimes—are black. Houston County, in which Dothan is located, has one of the highest numbers of death row prisoners per capita in the country—many of them black. Yet the county has never had a black district attorney, and the juries are almost solely white. "There's no justice system, for real, here in Houston County," says Raheimi Kinsey, who was sentenced to prison for robbing a convenience store. "The law does whatever they want to do, and we just have to accept it."[23]

The victim's race can also increase a black defendant's likelihood of getting the death penalty. Studies have found that an African American who kills a white person is more likely to get the death penalty than a black person who kills another black person, or a white person who kills someone of any race. "Blacks are most likely to pay the ultimate price when their victims are white," says David Jacobs, a researcher and professor of sociology at Ohio State University. "The disparity in execution rates based on the race of victims suggests our justice system places greater value on white lives, even after sentences are handed down."[24]

> "The disparity in execution rates based on the race of victims suggests our justice system places greater value on white lives, even after sentences are handed down."[24]
>
> —David Jacobs, researcher and professor of sociology, Ohio State University

Geography Matters

Further proof that the death penalty is not applied fairly is the fact that receiving the death penalty largely depends on where one lives. As of 2017, thirty-one states had the death penalty—most of them in the South and West. Consider that since 1976, 1,126 executions have been carried out in the South, while only 4 have been carried out in the Northeast. Also consider that just 2 percent of counties in the United States account for 52 percent of all capital punishment cases. This geographic disparity means that someone who commits murder in a northern state will likely receive a life sentence, while someone who commits the exact same crime in the South would more likely be executed.

Executing the Innocent

Uneven application of the death penalty is not the only way it is unfairly imposed. In its haste to solve crimes and serve justice, the overworked and underfunded justice system can sometimes make mistakes. Innocent people have ended up on death row, which is proved by the fact that many capital sentences have been overturned. One exmple is the case of Juan Roberto Meléndez-Colón, who spent more than seventeen years on death row before his innocence was proved and he was released. However, Meléndez-Colón was lucky; it is likely not every mistake is caught. This would mean that innocent people have probably been executed. Such a situation is unacceptable for any society that purports to be just and fair. "You can always release an innocent person from prison," says Meléndez-Colón, who himself was finally released in 2002, "but you can never release an innocent man from the grave."[25]

> "You can always release an innocent person from prison, but you can never release an innocent man from the grave."[25]
>
> —Juan Roberto Meléndez-Colón, who was sentenced to death in 1984 but was exonerated and released in 2002

A 2014 study in the *Proceedings of the National Academy of Sciences* concluded that about 4.1 percent of people who are sentenced to death are actually innocent. The authors of the study say the real number could be even higher, because not every wrongful conviction is caught. "It's a warning, an objective look at how we have been successful in finding some of these cases, but probably we're missing a lot," says Richard Dieter, executive director of the Death Penalty Information Center, a nonprofit organization that educates the public about capital punishment. "It raises the ultimate question of: Do we keep doing this?"[26]

DNA Testing Is Not a Fail-Safe

Former US Marine Kirk Bloodsworth was sentenced to death in 1985 for the rape and murder of a nine-year-old girl. In 1993, after spending nine years in prison, he became the first person to be exonerated (proved innocent) using DNA evidence. Since then, hundreds of other convictions have been overturned due to DNA evidence and other factors. It is hard to know how many people have been wrongfully executed, because prosecutors often destroy case files after an execution, and legal aid groups do not have the time or funding to go back and investigate the cases of people who have already been killed.

Since DNA evidence came into use in the late 1980s, it has improved the certainty of criminal convictions. Yet DNA evidence is not available in every case, and even when it is, it is not foolproof. "The DNA 'truth-machine' is only useful in a tiny sliver of criminal cases, and these are mostly not death penalty cases,"[27] says Brandon Garrett, a professor at the University of Virginia School of Law. DNA testing is expensive and time-consuming, and the results can be subject to bias, depending on who reviews the evidence. The fallibility of DNA evidence, along with the death penalty's uneven and discriminatory application, should make all Americans question the wisdom of using capital punishment.

Chapter Three

Is the Death Penalty Ethical?

The Death Penalty Is Ethical

- People who commit murder give up their right to live; they do not deserve sympathy, compassion, or comfort.
- Capital punishment does not negate the value of life—it confirms life's value by doling out the most extreme punishment for killing.
- The death penalty is ethical because it upholds the "eye for an eye" concept of justice authorized by the Bible.
- The death penalty is not vengeful because it is guided by law and carried out by representatives of the state, not victims.

The Debate at a Glance

The Death Penalty Is Unethical

- The death penalty constitutes cruel and unusual punishment, which is prohibited by the US Constitution.
- Executions cause more death and suffering, create more bereaved people, and compound suffering—all of which is unethical.
- The death penalty fails to address the social problems that drive murder, and thus is reactionary and unproductive.
- Capital punishment brings the government down to the level of the criminal and puts the United States in the company of the world's worst human rights abusers.

The Death Penalty Is Ethical

"We have the responsibility to punish those who deserve it. . . . The retributive punishment fits the crime."

—Robert Blecker, New York Law School professor

Quoted in *Dallas News*, "Q&A: Death Penalty Proponent Robert Blecker," April 2014. www.dallasnews.com.

Consider these questions as you read:

1. Is it ethical to make someone suffer death if they committed murder? Why or why not?
2. In your opinion, does the death penalty affirm or negate the value of life? Explain your reasoning.
3. Do you think biblical passages that support the death penalty justify imposing this form of punishment? Why or why not?

Editor's note: The discussion that follows presents common arguments made in support of this perspective, reinforced by facts, quotes, and examples taken from various sources.

When murderers takes an innocent life, it is perfectly ethical that they forfeit their own right to live. People who are guilty of the most heinous crimes deserve to be punished in a way that reflects the crime they committed.

Murderers Get What They Deserve

Consider the case of Brett Pensinger, who in 1981 kidnapped, tortured, and killed a five-month-old girl named Michelle Melander. The girl's tiny body was cut to pieces, and her skull was shattered. Pensinger had done unspeakable things to Melander, including cutting into her abdomen to remove her uterus.

Or, take David Allen Lucas, a carpet cleaner from California. In 1984 Lucas murdered two women and a three-year-old boy. Lucas slashed the victims' throats so deeply that some of them were nearly decapitated. Prosecutor Daniel Williams said the killings were "the most vicious and coldblooded murders San Diego has ever had to suffer."[28] The judge in the case said there was nothing heard or presented during the trial "to support sympathy or mercy for (Lucas) in light of the crimes."[29]

Death is the only appropriate and ethical punishment for monsters like Lucas and Pensinger. The alternative to the death penalty is that these men live out their lives in prison, an experience funded by taxpayers. This is a deeply unethical use of public money and also makes a mockery of the concept of justice. "While there are certainly costs to keeping death row inmates locked up and executed, it's worth every penny," says former California state senator Phil Wyman. "These dangerous individuals do not deserve the luxury of a long life at taxpayer expense and the benefit of breathing while so many of their victims, including countless children, lie in the ground."[30] Indeed, it would be unethical to allow murderers to continue to experience life—even prison life—when their victims have no such chance.

> "These dangerous individuals do not deserve the luxury of a long life at taxpayer expense and the benefit of breathing while so many of their victims, including countless children, lie in the ground."[30]
>
> —Former California state senator Phil Wyman

Capital Punishment Confirms the Value of Life

By executing a murderer, society does not negate the value of life—it confirms that value. By executing those who have killed, society in effect says that life is precious; only good people deserve to experience it. Thus, the death penalty is ethical because it affirms the sanctity of life. Moreover, those who criticize the death penalty as inhumane critically misunderstand its essence. "By seeking the death penalty, it is important to remember that it is not a reflection of *our* brutality, but rather an expression of our disdain for *their* brutal actions,"[31] explains Michael Ramos, district attorney in San Bernardino, California.

Why the Death Penalty Is Not Vengeful

Some criticize the death penalty as being uncivilized; they claim it is more about vengeance than meting out justice. However, the way the death penalty is handed out in contemporary society proves this to be untrue. When murderers are sentenced to death, they are done so by a jury of their peers according to a set of legal guidelines. The process is also overseen by a judge. Therefore, there are no personal feelings involved in the process. The death penalty could rightfully be called vengeful if, say, the murdered person's family were allowed to kill the guilty person in a manner of the family's choosing. Of course, the modern justice system allows no such thing. An impartial judge and jury handing down a legally sanctioned and uniformly designed death penalty sentence is simply a punishment that suits the severity of the crime.

> "By seeking the death penalty, it is important to remember that it is not a reflection of *our* brutality, but rather an expression of our disdain for *their* brutal actions."[31]
>
> —Michael Ramos, district attorney in San Bernardino, California

In fact, the presence of the death penalty removes the possibility that the public will take matters of the law into their own hands. That is what lynch mobs did in the South and Old West in the 1800s, which certainly constituted unethical punishment. In contrast, legal retribution is an orderly and ethical way to punish serious crimes.

It Is Wrong to Treat Murderers Humanely

That said, some contemporary death penalty methods are actually too compassionate for the worst killers. Methods of capital punishment have become more humane over the years, which is wrong, given what murderers have done.

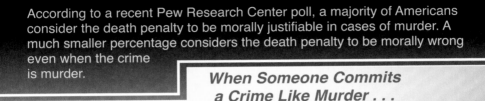

Americans View the Death Penalty as a Moral Response to Murder

According to a recent Pew Research Center poll, a majority of Americans consider the death penalty to be morally justifiable in cases of murder. A much smaller percentage considers the death penalty to be morally wrong even when the crime is murder.

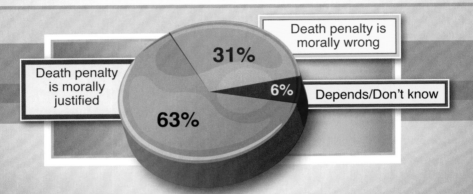

When Someone Commits a Crime Like Murder . . .

Death penalty is morally wrong

Death penalty is morally justified

31%

63%

6% Depends/Don't know

Source: Pew Research Center, "Less Support for Death Penalty, Especially Among Democrats," April 16, 2015. www.people-press.org.

Consider lethal injection, in which a murderer dies by receiving a fatal dose of medication. The injection is administered by someone with medical training, and a doctor or medical technician confirms the death when it occurs. To onlookers, this is seen as a calm and quiet way to die. However, this sanitized, tranquil death is too good for people who terrified, tortured, and viciously killed their victims. "How we kill those we rightly detest should in no way resemble how we end the suffering of those we love,"[32] says Professor Robert Blecker.

Blecker is right—it is completely ethical for murderers to suffer during an execution, and actually unethical if they don't; after all, they made their victims suffer. A painless death for a perpetrator is deeply unfair to his or her victims. This is why Blecker and others argue that so-called humane death penalty methods should be abolished and replaced with more straightforward executions. "The firing squad, among all traditional methods, probably serves us best," says Blecker. "It does not sugarcoat, it does not pretend, it does not shamefully obscure what we do. We kill them, intentionally, because they deserve it."[33]

Efforts to abolish the death penalty reveal a misplaced compassion for perpetrators. Consider how in July 2014, the state of Arizona executed Joseph R. Wood III for the 1989 murders of Debra Dietz and her father, Eugene. The execution was described by many as "botched." During it, Wood struggled to breathe for two hours while receiving the injection, which had to be administered fifteen times. Many argued that Wood's execution was tantamount to cruel and unusual punishment, and some described it as "excruciating." However, was Wood's experience really so undeserved, considering what he did to his victims? Indeed, the Dietz family was rightfully outraged by the sympathy the public seemed to have for their loved ones' murderer. "You don't know what excruciating is," said Debra Dietz's sister, Jeannie Brown. "What is excruciating is seeing your dad laying there in a pool of blood, seeing your sister there in a pool of blood." Her husband, Richard, added, "You know, these people that do this, that are on death row, they deserve to suffer a little bit."[34]

The Death Penalty Fulfills "an Eye for an Eye"

The death penalty has its roots in biblical concepts of justice, which further confirms its morality. The biblical phrase "an eye for an eye" is based on the premise of equal retaliation. It makes clear that a person who commits a crime deserves a similar penalty in response. This makes it acceptable to kill someone who has killed. Elsewhere in the Bible this idea is confirmed. Genesis reads, "Whoever sheds the blood of man, by man shall his blood be shed."[35]

Murderers have forfeited their place among the living; they do not deserve to experience anything life has to offer, including our compassion. Clearly the death penalty is an ethical way to respond to the worst actions imaginable.

The Death Penalty Is Unethical

"A society that respects life does not deliberately kill human beings. An execution is a violent public spectacle of official homicide, and one that endorses killing to solve social problems."

—American Civil Liberties Union (ACLU)

American Civil Liberties Union, "The Case Against the Death Penalty," ACLU.org, April 2014. www.aclu.org.

Consider these questions as you read:

1. In your opinion, does capital punishment qualify as cruel and unusual punishment? Why or why not?
2. How does knowing which countries execute the most prisoners influence your opinion of whether the death penalty is moral?
3. Does the death penalty's cost influence your opinion of whether it is ethical? Why or why not?

Editor's note: The discussion that follows presents common arguments made in support of this perspective, reinforced by facts, quotes, and examples taken from various sources.

The death penalty is the ultimate denial of human rights. It violates human dignity and is a form of cruel and unusual punishment, which is prohibited under the Eighth Amendment of the US Constitution. While it may be satisfying or instinctive to punish a murderer with death, a closer look reveals that doing so is illogical and unethical.

The Death Penalty Is Immoral Because It Is Torture

No matter what execution method is used—electrocution, the gas chamber, hanging, or firing squad—execution is extremely painful. To reduce this agony, states today use lethal injection for most executions, a method once thought of as fast and relatively painless. However, people are increasingly realizing this is not the case.

Consider what happened in 2014 when the state of Oklahoma executed convicted killer Clayton Lockett. It took several needle sticks to administer the first drug, and the attending doctor was spattered with so much blood that the prison warden described the scene as "a bloody mess."[36] Finally, Lockett seemed to fall asleep. But once another drug was injected, he began to writhe, buck, and moan on the gurney. "It was like a horror movie," says Edith Shoals, a victim services advocate who witnessed the execution. "He kept trying to talk."[37] In the end it took almost an hour to complete an execution that should have taken just minutes.

Lockett's execution is one of many that have been considered "botched." These experiences have led to increased calls to outlaw lethal injection and the death penalty itself. In fact, the botched lethal injection of a criminal named Dennis McGuire in 2014 caused the State of Ohio to put a three-year moratorium on the practice.

Interestingly, even companies that make drugs used in lethal injections have protested using them for this purpose. In 2016, Pfizer, which makes a sedative that was widely used in lethal injections, put in place restrictions that prevent its product from being used for that purpose. "Their business is in making medicines to save and improve the lives of patients," explains Maya Foa, director of Reprieve, a human rights organization. "The last thing they want is for the medicines they promote as lifesaving to be used in lethal-injection executions."[38]

> "Capital punishment is under all circumstances cruel and unusual punishment."[39]
>
> —Former Supreme Court justice William J. Brennan

Cruel and Unusual Punishment

Botched executions that create suffering sound a lot like cruel and unusual punishment, which the United States has declared to be not only unethical but also illegal. No less a legal scholar than the late Supreme

Court justice William J. Brennan has viewed the death penalty in this light. "As I interpret the Constitution, capital punishment is under all circumstances cruel and unusual punishment,"[39] he said. "It treats members of the human race as nonhumans, as objects to be toyed with and discarded. It is, indeed, 'cruel and unusual.'"[40] Brennan suggests that even the most horrific act by a criminal does not release the state from its responsibility to uphold human rights and the Constitution.

Even spending years on death row is itself a form of cruel and unusual punishment. Inmates sit in solitary confinement for up to twenty-three hours a day, waiting to find out if and when they will be executed. "There is an enormous agony in endlessly, and helplessly, waiting while others decide whether you live or die,"[41] says psychiatrist Stuart Grassian.

Execution Creates More Death, Injustice, and Suffering

The death penalty not only creates suffering for the one being executed, but it makes that person's family suffer as well, which is another reason it is immoral. Even though sympathy is rarely extended to the family of the executed, they too suffer when their loved one is killed. "You'll never hear another sound like a mother wailing when she is watching her son be executed,"[42] said one warden. By creating more pain and grief for those who are bereaved, the death penalty merely compounds misery.

In addition, consider that most people who are sentenced to death have usually themselves been victims. Many who are sentenced to die endured childhoods filled with abuse. For example, Lockett was sexually abused by his half-brother, and his father beat him with anything he could get his hands on, from belts to wooden boards.

From this vantage point, the death penalty is merely an unethical response to an immoral situation. Killing someone like Lockett only adds to the injustice the victim has already experienced. It never gives these victims an opportunity to redeem themselves, reform, or make amends for the crime they have committed. It also doesn't address the societal problems that turned people like Lockett into killers. As a civilized and compassionate society, America should care about the plight of such people and support ways to prevent such brutalization from happening

America Is in Poor Company When It Comes to the Death Penalty

The United States consistently has a place at the table of unethical nations—those that are most frequently cited for human rights abuses—thanks to its continued use of the death penalty. According to Amnesty International, in 2016 the United States once again joined countries such as China, Iran, Saudi Arabia, and Iraq on the list of nations that carried out the most executions. The United States placed seventh on that list in 2016. This is marginally better than 2015, when the United States was listed in the top five.

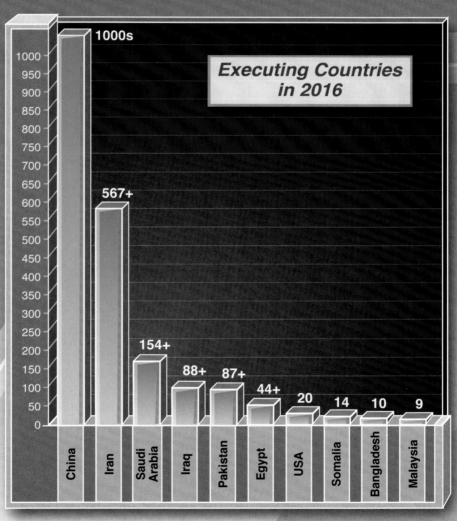

Executing Countries in 2016

China	1000s
Iran	567+
Saudi Arabia	154+
Iraq	88+
Pakistan	87+
Egypt	44+
USA	20
Somalia	14
Bangladesh	10
Malaysia	9

Source: Amnesty International, "Death Sentences and Executions, 2016," Amnesty International Global Report, 2017. www.amnesty.org.

in the first place. In the case of Lockett, more useful than the death penalty would have been stronger laws that protect children from abuse and mistreatment.

Capital Punishment Has No Place in Civilized Society

Capital punishment brings the government down to the level of the criminal. It also puts the United States in the company of several countries that are widely recognized as undemocratic and violators of human rights. In 2015 most of the world's executions took place in five countries: China, Iran, Pakistan, Saudi Arabia—and the United States. In contrast, the majority of democracies—including most countries in Europe, which are among America's strongest allies—have outlawed the death penalty. How can the United States claim to support human rights when it adopts practices used by the world's worst abusers of those rights?

Religions Oppose the Death Penalty

Along with human rights advocates, many religions oppose the death penalty, which further indicates that it is unethical. Most Jews favor either abolishing the practice or pausing its use. Buddhists promote ideals of nonviolence and respect for life. Christianity preaches forgiveness. In fact, the United States Conference of Catholic Bishops (USCCB) has called for the abolishment of capital punishment because it believes that no sin is too great to be forgiven. "There are as many degrees of guilt and culpability as there are crimes, yet the death penalty imposes one definitive, final, indiscriminate punishment on all, halting the action of the Holy Spirit on the condemned person's soul for eternity,"[43] the USCCB has said. Finally, the Bible makes a clear case against the death penalty when it commands, "Thou shalt not kill."

The High Cost of Death

However, one does not need to be spiritual to oppose the death penalty. There are financial issues that make the death penalty immoral as well. Capital punishment is enormously costly, and it is deeply unethical to waste this money when so many other programs and causes need funding. One such cause would be the prevention of childhood abuse that can turn children into killers later in life. Spending money on such a cause would surely be more ethical than spending it on the executions of those who were so victimized.

Death penalty cases can cost three to four times more than a non–death penalty case. It costs more to incarcerate someone on death row because such inmates typically require more security (so facilities where they are housed must be built differently), more supervision (so more guards must be hired), and more isolation (which means more money is spent per prisoner).

Defendants also need additional lawyers because capital cases feature numerous appeals. The appeals, petitions, and other legal exercises to ensure a convicted person is actually guilty can add up to millions of dollars more than the system would have spent imprisoning the person for life. For example, a 2015 study by Seattle University found that in Washington State, the average death penalty case costs $3.07 million, compared to $2.01 million for a non-capital case. American taxpayers usually fund these extra costs.

> "An evil deed is not redeemed by an evil deed of retaliation. Justice is never advanced in the taking of a human life. Morality is never upheld by a legalized murder."[44]
>
> —Activist and civil rights leader Coretta Scott King

Legalized Murder Is Still Murder

Taking a life does not erase the crime committed. Nor does it address the issues that lead murderers to kill. It only wastes money and creates more suffering. The death penalty clearly is not ethical. As activist and civil rights leader Coretta Scott King once said, "An evil deed is not redeemed by an evil deed of retaliation. Justice is never advanced in the taking of a human life. Morality is never upheld by a legalized murder."[44] Responding to murder with murder is unethical and counterproductive to solving the social problems that drive murder in the first place.

Chapter Four

Does the Death Penalty Serve Justice?

The Death Penalty Serves Justice

- Executing a murderer ends the long nightmare for victims' families and gives them a sense of closure.
- Capital punishment makes it impossible for convicted criminals to kill again—which they often do.
- Once criminals are executed, Americans no longer have to pay the exorbitant costs of their housing and care.

The Debate at a Glance

The Death Penalty Does Not Serve Justice

- Execution does not bring closure or a sense of justice to victims' families, in part because it takes so long to achieve.
- The appeals process forces families to relive the grisly details of their loved one's death over and over again.
- The death penalty makes victims out of the family of the executed.
- It is unjust to deny humans the chance to rehabilitate themselves, and society misses out on rehabilitated criminals' potential contributions when it executes them.

The Death Penalty Serves Justice

"There are cases where a dangerous criminal has escaped or found a legal means to roam free and kill again, but once a killer is dead—that's the end of their threat to society. Period."

—Garry Rodgers, former homicide detective and forensic coroner

Garry Rodgers, "Capital Punishment—Justice or State Sanctioned Murder?," *Huffington Post*, January 21, 2016. www.huffingtonpost.com.

Consider these questions as you read:

1. Would the execution of a loved one's killer offer you a sense of closure and justice? Why or why not?
2. Can you think of a way to ensure a murderer does not kill again that does not involve executing him or her?
3. In your opinion, is it unfair for Americans to pay such high costs to incarcerate the worst criminals? Why or why not?

Editor's note: The discussion that follows presents common arguments made in support of this perspective, reinforced by facts, quotes, and examples taken from various sources.

The United States should retain the death penalty for many reasons, including that it is fair, humane, and ethical. But above all, the death penalty is an appropriate and just response to the greatest injustice that exists—the murder of an innocent person. When such a terrible event occurs, the death penalty is the only mechanism by which to offer justice to families, to communities, and to all of society.

The Death Penalty Provides Closure

First and foremost, the death penalty serves justice to the family members of murder victims. It gives them the closure they need and the peace they deserve. This is how the family of Sean Collier felt in May 2015, when a federal jury sentenced Boston Marathon bomber Dzhokhar Tsarnaev to death. Two years earlier, Tsarnaev and his brother, Tamerlan, exploded two bombs along the route of the Boston Marathon, killing three people and injuring hundreds of others. Collier was a twenty-six-year-old police officer killed in the attack. While his family will never recover from their horrific loss, knowing Tsarnaev would be denied the opportunity to live offered them some measure of comfort. "While today's verdict can never bring Sean back, we are thankful that Dzhokhar Tsarnaev will be held accountable for the evil that he brought to so many families,"[45] they said.

> "We are thankful that Dzhokhar Tsarnaev will be held accountable for the evil that he brought to so many families."[45]
>
> —The family of Sean Collier, who was killed in the Boston Marathon bombing

For victims' families, putting a murderer to death ends the long nightmare that began with the crime and continued through a lengthy trial. Capital punishment finally gives survivors like Anita Hayes a chance to move beyond their pain. Hayes's niece and her niece's two children were murdered by Caron E. Montgomery in 2010. When Montgomery's death sentence was announced in court, Hayes and other family members shouted, "Yes! Yes!" in relief. "I can't imagine what the death penalty is for if not for this," said Hayes, who also added that the family "felt comforted to know that he will be put to death."[46]

Protecting Public Safety

Another way in which the death penalty provides justice is that it permanently incapacitates those who most threaten society. If a killer remains alive, even in prison, he or she is capable of killing again. And convicted murderers do kill again—other inmates and prison guards are among their victims. Donna Payant, a corrections officer at Green Haven Correctional Facility in New York, was killed by Lemuel Smith in 1981. Smith was already serving two life sentences for murdering and raping other victims when he cornered Payant in a secluded area of the prison.

Killing Killers Saves Lives

Not all killers are sentenced to die. Some serve their sentences and then are released. And some of these individuals go on to kill again. This is why many people believe that the death penalty serves justice; it prevents killers from killing again.

Name	First offense	Year Paroled	Second Offense
John Miller	**1957** Killed 22-month-old girl	**1975**	**1975** Killed his parents
John McRae	**1951** Killed an 8-year-old boy	**1972**	**1987** Killed a 15-year-old boy
Jimmy Lee Gray	**1968** Killed his 16-year-old girlfriend	**1970s**	**1976** Killed a 3-year-old girl
Corey R. Barton	**1983** Killed a 16-year-old girl	**1992**	**1998** Killed his ex-girlfriend
Howard Allen	**1974** Killed an 85-year-old woman	**1984**	**1998** Killed two women, aged 73 and 87
Dwaine Little	**1964** Killed a 16-year-old girl	**1974**	**1980** Killed a pregnant hitchhiker
Arthur Shawcross	**1972** Killed an 8-year-old girl	**1987**	**1980s** Killed eleven women
Timothy Buss	**1981** Killed a 5-year-old girl	**1993**	**1995** Killed a 10-year-old boy
Robert Lee Massie	**1965** Killed 48-year-old woman	**1978**	**1979** Killed a 61-year-old liquor store clerk

Source: James Wray, "10 Twisted Murderers Who Were Freed Then Killed Again," Monsters and Critics, July 2, 2016.

He strangled her and dumped her body in a sanitation compactor. It is heartbreaking to think that Payant would be alive today had Smith been given the death penalty instead of life in prison.

Convicted murderers can have victims outside the prison, too. A victim's family constantly needs to worry about the possibility that a murderer will be paroled or accidentally released, or escape from prison. While some think this is farfetched, it happens more often than people think. According to the Associated Press, in 2015 there were 220 escaped prisoners at large across the United States. Several were convicted murderers. Victims' families should not have to live in fear that their loved one's murderer might one day come for them.

Once freed from prison, offenders can and do commit more violent offenses. Steven Pratt was fifteen years old when he shot and killed his next-door neighbor. He served twenty-eight years in prison and was released in October 2014. Just two days later, he beat his mother to death during an argument. Had he been executed for his original crime of killing his neighbor, his mother would still be alive.

These stories are not isolated cases. In fact, according to the Bureau of Justice Statistics, 71 percent of violent offenders recidivate—meaning they commit another crime—within five years of their release. About half of these offenders originally committed murder. When a violent criminal is released, all of society is at risk. The only way to eliminate that risk is to make it impossible for killers to kill again. As retired homicide detective Garry Rodgers puts it, "It's an indisputable fact that execution guarantees that [a] person will never re-offend."[47]

It Is Unjust for Murderers to Live on Taxpayer Money

Finally, executing killers swiftly is the only way to ensure they do not unjustly cost taxpayers money. When a killer is sentenced to prison—either for a few years or for life—taxpayers foot the bill to house, feed, clothe, and otherwise care for that inmate. According to the US Bureau of Prisons, the average cost of incarcerating a prisoner is nearly $31,000 per year. Therefore, it costs about $620,000 to house an inmate who has a twenty-year prison sentence, and a whopping $1.24 million to house someone with a forty-year sentence. American taxpayers are responsible for these costs, including the victims' families, who are put in the awful position of paying to house, feed, and clothe the person who murdered their loved one.

Now consider that it usually costs more to house death row inmates than prisoners in a regular facility. This is because death row inmates have been deemed so dangerous they are kept in individual cells. They also require more supervision, which results in higher costs for security infrastructure and guard personnel salaries. In fact, a 2014 study done on prisons in Kansas found that it costs about twice as much to house a death row prisoner (about $49,000 per year) than someone in the general population (about $24,000 per year).

The costs of housing death row inmates would not be a problem if the death penalty were swiftly enacted. Unfortunately, in many states inmates destined for execution often sit on death row for many years. The Bureau of Justice Statistics reports that as of 2017, the average length of stay on death row was 16.8 years. Moreover, many death row inmates actually end up dying not from execution, but of old age and natural causes. One such

> "It's an indisputable fact that execution guarantees that [a] person will never re-offend."[47]
>
> —Garry Rodgers, retired homicide detective

person is Gary Alvord, a three-time murderer who spent forty years on Florida's death row before he finally died of old age in 2013. Another is Brandon Astor Jones, who murdered someone in 1979. More than thirty-five years later, at seventy-two years old, Jones was still awaiting execution. In fact, in 2011, twenty-four death row prisoners around the country died of natural causes.

If death penalty sentences were handed out in a timely manner, states could avoid overspending on the people who deserve it least. As it currently stands, however, the nation's worst criminals live best and at the highest cost. "Our most violent criminals, those who would be legally deserving of the death penalty, require the most resources to pay for their high security cells and 'extended' stays in our nation's jails,"[48] writes Princeton University student Chris Goodnow. Professor Robert Blecker agrees. He has spent months comparing prison life across several states and different kinds of security facilities. "The perverse irony [is] this," he writes. "Inside prisons, often the worst criminals live the most comfortable lives . . . while the relatively petty criminals live miserably."[49]

It is a travesty of justice that murderers live for so many years beyond their convictions, and at such high cost. This, coupled with the fact that the death penalty offers closure to victims' families and permanently incapacitates criminals, is among the many reasons why the death penalty is the best punishment for serving justice.

The Death Penalty Does Not Serve Justice

"More often than not, families of murder victims do not experience the relief they expected to feel at the execution. . . . Taking a life doesn't fill that void, but it's generally not until after the execution that families realize this."

—Lula Redmond, certified death educator and bereavement counselor

Quoted in Robert T. Muller, "Death Penalty May Not Bring Peace to Victims' Families," *Psychology Today*, October 19, 2016. www.psychologytoday.com.

Consider these questions as you read:

1. What factors prevent victims' families from feeling closure in death penalty cases?
2. Do you think it is possible for convicted murderers to ever be truly rehabilitated? Explain your reasoning.
3. In your opinion, should the family members of murder victims have a say in the sentencing if they feel the death penalty is unjustified? Why or why not?

Editor's note: The discussion that follows presents common arguments made in support of this perspective, reinforced by facts, quotes, and examples taken from various sources.

Capital punishment exists because of the notion that it is a just punishment for a horrible crime. However, a closer look at the emotional effects of the death penalty on victims' families, on convicted murderers, and on the families of the executed suggests it is not just at all.

Closure Is an Illusion

One of the most emotional claims of death penalty supporters is that executions bring closure to victims' families. Yet many families do not feel any sense of relief after an execution. Closure itself is a term that is hard to define because it means different things to different people. To some, *closure* might simply mean knowing who killed their loved one. To others, it can mean putting the murderer in prison for life. Not every family, in other words, would seek a remedy as final as an execution to find closure.

In any case, even with its sense of finality, the death penalty does not put an end to grief. The victims' loved ones continue to suffer long after a murderer is executed. "In many capital cases, victims' families are given false hope that their pain will go away with an execution," says Drake University sociology professor Nancy Berns. "They may be relieved to have the trial behind them, but their pain and grief will still be part of the journey."[50]

> "In many capital cases, victims' families are given false hope that their pain will go away with an execution. They may be relieved to have the trial behind them, but their pain and grief will still be part of the journey."[50]
>
> —Nancy Berns, professor of sociology, Drake University

Prolonging the Agony

If anything, the years of appeals and other hearings that follow a death sentence can prolong family members' agony, forcing them to relive the grisly details of a loved one's death over and over again. They are required to hear of a crime's details before multiple courts and offer gut-wrenching testimony to numerous juries.

This is what family members of Dylann Roof's victims must endure. On June 17, 2015, Roof shot and killed nine churchgoers in Charleston, South Carolina. "Family members of his victims will have to suffer through not one but two trials, because South Carolina and the federal government are bringing duplicative charges," notes Tanya Coke,

There Is No Justice When Innocent People Are Condemned to Die

Since 1973, according to the Death Penalty Information Center, 158 death row inmates have been exonerated of crimes and freed. This leads to the obvious question: How many others have been executed for crimes they did not commit? Almost fourteen hundred individuals have been executed in the United States since 1976. There is no way to know whether any of these people were innocent of the crimes for which they died but even one innocent person being executed is a clear miscarriage of justice.

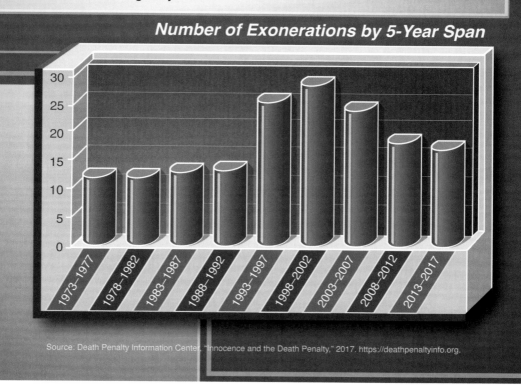

Number of Exonerations by 5-Year Span

Source: Death Penalty Information Center, "Innocence and the Death Penalty," 2017. https://deathpenaltyinfo.org.

a former defense attorney and criminal justice expert. "And because a death sentence by law requires review by an appellate court, the family members of the Charleston victims will have to face years—most likely decades—of appeals and accompanying news stories that will reopen old wounds."[51] The family members of Roof's victims do not want to endlessly relive their most painful memories.

This was exactly the sentiment expressed by the family of eight-year-old Martin Richard, the youngest victim of the 2013 Boston Marathon bombing. In fact, the Richards' family argued against giving the death penalty to Dzhokhar Tsarnaev, who along with his brother killed three people and injured hundreds. "We know that the government has its reasons for seeking the death penalty, but the continued pursuit of that punishment could bring years of appeals and prolong reliving the most painful day of our lives,"[52] they wrote.

More Solace in Forgiveness

Many family members of murder victims see the death penalty as a kind of revenge, and they are not comfortable with the idea of taking another life. "For a growing number of victims of violence, the thought of honoring our loved ones by killing another human being is not only counter-intuitive, but abhorrent,"[53] says Coke. On the contrary, murder victims' families want to feel whole again, but they rarely get that relief from the death penalty. In fact, a 2012 Marquette University study found that victims' families had better physical and mental health when juries handed out life sentences to perpetrators, rather than capital punishment. This is because many family members find more solace in forgiveness than in retribution.

> "The thought of honoring our loved ones by killing another human being is not only counter-intuitive, but abhorrent."[53]
>
> —Tanya Coke, former defense attorney

Consider Gayle Orr, whose nineteen-year-old daughter was stabbed to death in 1980. After the murderer was executed, Orr entered what she referred to as a "period of darkness." Only after she had written a letter of forgiveness to her daughter's killer did she start to heal. "The instant that I put that letter in the mailbox," she says, "all the anger, all the rage, all the darkness that I've been carrying around, all the ugliness I've been carrying around in my body for 12 long years, instantly was gone. Just gone. And in its place I was filled with this sense of joy and love."[54]

Stanford University psychiatrist David Spiegel says that this is because real closure "is achieved only through extensive grief work."[55] This process includes talking to counselors and coming to terms with the loss. This is exactly why Tanya Coke says she would prefer to talk to Dylann Roof about his childhood, what caused him to kill, and whether he ever thinks about his victims. Humanizing him would help her hate him less, and hate is not an emotion she wants inside her. "The death penalty requires all of us, victims and spectators alike, to actively summon feelings of hatred and contempt in order to justify the murder of another human being," she says. "But I know one thing for certain: They aren't emotions I want to hang on to. I'm old enough to understand that hate is a cancerous emotion that hurts me more than it hurts [a killer]."[56]

Pain for the Accused's Family

The capital punishment process also brings great pain to the perpetrator's family. They, like the victim's family, have to revisit the terrible details of the case again and again with each trial. It is also awful for them to witness their loved one's execution. One warden described the agonizing screams that mothers of the executed let out as they watch their son or daughter be killed by the state. "There's no other sound like it," he says. "It is just this horrendous wail. It's definitely something you won't ever forget."[57]

Some people are reluctant to extend sympathy to murderers' families, but these mothers, fathers, brothers, sisters, husbands, wives, and children are themselves innocent victims of a crime. "The shock that comes with a death sentence can leave the family members quite vulnerable to developing emotional and mental disorders," writes author Sandra Joy in her book, *Grief, Loss, and Treatment for Death Row Families*. "The grief that they feel from losing their loved one to death row and the horror they imagine is yet to come as the state sets out to follow through on their plans to execute their loved one can be truly overwhelming."[58] Once the execution takes place, the family members of the executed have something in common with the family members of the victims—both have lost people important to them to murder.

Rehabilitation Is Possible

Supporters of the death penalty often argue that murderers cannot be rehabilitated, so execution is the only way to ensure they do not kill again. However, this is flawed and harsh reasoning. Many convicted murderers can be rehabilitated, and executing them steals from them the chance to change.

Consider Jesse Reed, who was convicted of first-degree murder in 1985. While high on drugs, he shot and killed a man during a robbery. Reed did a lot of self-reflecting in prison. He experienced extreme remorse for his crime and went through several phases of grief and self-punishment. After serving twenty-seven years of a potential life sentence, Reed was deemed rehabilitated and paroled. He now participates in a state-run program in which he counsels young inmates. Had he been executed, society would have lost the chance to benefit from his contributions. "Today I'm an individual who decided that he wanted to change," says Reed. "Change comes from within. It's just having a desire to be better."[59]

Reed is like many other convicted murderers who do not kill again. Journalist Nancy Mullane has extensively investigated the issue of recidivism by working with Reed and other convicted murderers in California. She found that of one thousand convicted murderers who were paroled from California's prisons between 1990 and 2011, zero committed another murder. While it is true that some murderers do kill again, the majority do not. Executing them all wastes the chance to find out what they are capable of giving back to society.

There Is No Justice in Death

Because it is final, cruel, and vengeful, the death penalty can never offer grieving families what they need: closure, peace, and justice. The only way to achieve this is by extending compassion and mercy to those who seem to deserve it least but in fact need it the most. The death penalty accomplishes nothing productive or healing. More often it just creates more misery, anger, and death—and there is no justice in that.

Source Notes

Overview: The Death Penalty

1. Quoted in Alan Blinder, "U.S. Seeks Death for Charleston Shooting Suspect. Victims' Families Prefer Mercy," *New York Times*, November 26, 2016. www.nytimes.com.
2. Quoted in Blinder, "U.S. Seeks Death for Charleston Shooting Suspect."
3. Quoted in P.J. Harland, *The Value of Human Life: A Study of the Story of the Flood (Genesis 6–9)*. Leiden, Netherlands: E.J. Brill, 1996.
4. Quoted in Hugo Bedau and Paul Cassell, eds., *Debating the Death Penalty*. New York: Oxford University Press, 2004, p. 16.
5. Quoted in Kenneth Williams, *Most Deserving of Death? An Analysis of the Supreme Court's Death Penalty Jurisprudence*. New York: Routledge, 2016.
6. Quoted in Bill of Rights Institute, *Gregg v. Georgia (1976)*. www.billof rightsinstitute.org.
7. Quoted in UN News Centre, "'Death Penalty Has No Place in 21st Century,' Declares UN Chief," July 2, 2014. www.un.org.

Chapter One: Does the Death Penalty Deter Crime?

8. David B. Muhlhausen, "How the Death Penalty Saves Lives," *U.S. News & World Report*, September 29, 2014. www.usnews.com.
9. Quoted in Mara Bovson, "Justice Story: How a Botched Bank Job for Sex-Change Loot Inspired the Classic 'Dog Day Afternoon,'" *New York Daily News*, August 18, 2012. www.nydailynews.com.
10. Quoted in Bedau and Cassell, eds., *Debating the Death Penalty*, p. 61.
11. Quoted in Lisa Goldberg, "Convicted Killer Charged in Recent Death," *Hartford (CT) Courant*, January 8, 1999. http://articles.courant.com.
12. Robert S. Henry, "The Death Penalty Is About Deterrence, Not Revenge," *Los Angeles Times,* November 7, 2016. www.latimes.com.
13. John Donohue, "Does the Death Penalty Deter Killers?," *Newsweek*, August 19, 2015. www.newsweek.com.
14. Quoted in Donohue, "Does the Death Penalty Deter Killers?"
15. Quoted in Max Ehrenfreund, "There's Still No Evidence That Executions Deter Criminals," *Washington Post,* April 30, 2014. www.washingtonpost .com.
16. Donohue, "Does the Death Penalty Deter Killers?"
17. Florence Bellivier and Dimitris Christopoulos, "Our Answer to Terrorism Cannot Be the Death Penalty," FIDH.org, October 10, 2016. www.fidh .org.
18. Quoted in Ehrenfreund, "There's Still No Evidence That Executions Deter Criminals."

Chapter Two: Is the Death Penalty Fairly Imposed?

19. Justice Scalia, "*Kansas v. Marsh* (No. 04-1170)," Legal Information Institute, Cornell University Law School, June 26, 2006. www.law.cornell.edu.
20. Scalia, "*Kansas v. Marsh* (No. 04-1170)."
21. Ernest van den Haag, "Capital Punishment Saves Innocent Lives." http://faculty.polytechnic.org/gfeldmeth/19.cpsaveslives.pdf.
22. NC Coalition for Alternatives to the Death Penalty, "Ronald Frye." https://nccadp.org/story/ronald-frye.
23. Quoted in Shaila Dewan and Andrew W. Lehren, "Alabama Prosecutor Sets the Penalties and Fills the Coffers," *New York Times,* December 13, 2016. www.nytimes.com.
24. Quoted in Jeff Grabmeier, "Study: Blacks Who Kill Whites Are Most Likely to Be Executed," Research News, The Ohio State University. https://researchnews.osu.edu/archive/dthrow.htm.
25. Quoted in Dana Littlefield, "Ex–Death Row Inmate Urges Californians to Repeal Death Penalty," *San Diego Union-Tribune,* October 20, 2016. www.sandiegouniontribune.com.
26. Quoted in Pema Levy, "One in 25 Sentenced to Death in the U.S. Is Innocent, Study Claims," *Newsweek*, April 28, 2014. www.newsweek.com.
27. Brandon Garrett, "Learning What We Can from DNA," *CATO Unbound*, March 5, 2012. www.cato-unbound.org.

Chapter Three: Is the Death Penalty Ethical?

28. Quoted in Susan Shroder, "Death Penalty Upheld in Throat-Slashing Serial Murders," *San Diego Union-Tribune*, August 22, 2014. www.sandiegouniontribune.com.
29. Quoted in Alan Abrahamson, "Lucas Sentenced to Die for 3 Slashing Murders," *Los Angeles Times*, September 20, 1989. http://articles.latimes.com.
30. Phil Wyman, "Wyman Op-Ed," Californians for Death Penalty Reform and Savings, November 8, 2016. https://noprop62yesprop66.com.
31. Michael Ramos, "Improve Death Penalty Process, Don't Abolish It," *San Bernardino (CA) Sun*, October 22, 2016. www.sbsun.com.
32. Robert Blecker, "With Death Penalty, Let Punishment Truly Fit the Crime," CNN.com, August 22, 2013. www.cnn.com.
33. Blecker, "With Death Penalty, Let Punishment Truly Fit the Crime."
34. Quoted in Craig Bannister, "Victims' Family Blasts Media for Sympathizing with Executed Murderer Instead of Those He Killed," *CNS News* (blog), July 24, 2014. www.cnsnews.com.
35. Quoted in David VanDrunen, *Divine Covenants and Moral Order: A Biblical Theology of Natural Law*. Grand Rapids, MI: William B. Eerdmans, 2014, p. 509.
36. Quoted in Katie Fretland, "Scene at Botched Oklahoma Execution of Clayton Lockett Was 'a Bloody Mess,'" *Guardian* (Manchester, UK), December 13, 2014. www.theguardian.com.

37. Quoted in Fretland, "Scene at Botched Oklahoma Execution of Clayton Lockett Was 'a Bloody Mess.'"

38. Quoted in Lincoln Caplan, "The End of the Open Market for Lethal-Injection Drugs," *New Yorker,* May 21, 2016. www.newyorker.com.

39. William J. Brennan Jr., "Speech Given at the Text and Teaching Symposium, Georgetown University, October 12, 1985, Washington, DC," Supreme Court History: The Court and Democracy, Primary Sources. www.pbs.org.

40. Brennan Jr., "Speech Given at the Text and Teaching Symposium."

41. Quoted in Michael J. Carter, "Waiting to Die: The Cruel Phenomenon of 'Death Row Syndrome,'" AlterNet, November 7, 2008. www.alternet.org.

42. Quoted in Laura Dimon, "Chilling Testimony of Death Row Executioners Casts Dark Shadow over Entire System," Mic, January 15, 2014. https://mic.com.

43. United States Conference of Catholic Bishops, "Life Matters: The Death Penalty," *Lay Witness Magazine,* January/February 2012. www.cuf.org.

44. Quoted in David A. Love, "Dr. King's Stance Against the Death Penalty," *Huffington Post,* January 16, 2012. www.huffingtonpost.com.

Chapter Four: Does the Death Penalty Serve Justice?

45. Quoted in Greg Botelho, Dorrine Mendoza, and Catherine E. Shoichet, "'One Step Closer to Closure': Boston Bombing Survivors React to Verdict," CNN.com, April 8, 2015. www.cnn.com.

46. Quoted in John Futty, "Death Penalty Brings Relief to Victims' Family," *Columbus (OH) Dispatch,* May 16, 2012. www.dispatch.com.

47. Garry Rodgers, "Capital Punishment—Justice or State Sanctioned Murder?," *Huffington Post,* January 21, 2016. www.huffingtonpost.com.

48. Chris Goodnow, "The Death Penalty Is a Just Punishment for the Most Heinous Crimes," *Princeton Tory,* December 11, 2011. http://theprincetontory.com.

49. Blecker, "With Death Penalty, Let Punishment Truly Fit the Crime."

50. Nancy Berns, "A Death Sentence Will Not Bring 'Closure,'" *Psychology Today,* May 15, 2015. www.psychologytoday.com.

51. Tanya Coke, "Death Penalty Punishes Survivors Like Me," *USA Today,* August 28, 2016. www.usatoday.com.

52. Quoted in Mark Sappenfield, "Dylann Roof and Death Penalty: Does It Matter What Victims' Families Want?," *Christian Science Monitor,* June 21, 2015. www.csmonitor.com.

53. Coke, "Death Penalty Punishes Survivors Like Me."

54. Quoted in Lisa Aliferis, "Does the Death Penalty Provide 'Closure' to Victim's Families? Three Perspectives," *KQED News* (blog), KQED, October 18, 2012. http://blogs.kqed.org.

55. Quoted in Naseem Rakha, "Do Executions Bring Closure?," *Washington Post,* November 10, 2009. www.washingtonpost.com.

56. Coke, "Death Penalty Punishes Survivors Like Me."
57. Quoted in Dimon, "Chilling Testimony of Death Row Executioners Casts Dark Shadow over Entire System."
58. Sandra Joy, *Grief, Loss, and Treatment for Death Row Families*. Lanham, MD: Lexington Books, 2014, pp. 110–11.
59. Quoted in "'After Murder': Learning to Live After You've Killed," NPR Author Interviews, July 7, 2012. www.npr.org.

Death Penalty Facts

History of the Death Penalty

- In 1846 Michigan became the first state to abolish the death penalty for all crimes but treason.
- In 1852 Rhode Island was the first state to do away with the death penalty entirely.
- After the 1972 *Furman v. Georgia* case, the Supreme Court suspended the death penalty.
- In 1976 the *Gregg v. Georgia* case reinstated the use of capital punishment.

Use of Capital Punishment

- As of 2017, more than half of all states authorized the use of the death penalty.
- In recent years, executions in the United States have been at their lowest levels in more than two decades.
- Most executions are carried out in the South.
- Just 2 percent of counties in the United States account for 52 percent of all death penalty cases.

Execution Methods

- People who were accused of a capital crime in ancient Greece or Rome were beaten, beheaded, burned, drowned at sea, crucified, fed to animals, or buried alive.
- In 1792 French physician Joseph-Ignace Guillotin invented the guillotine as a less painful method of execution.
- In 1890 the electric chair was invented with the help of Thomas Edison.
- Lethal injection became a method of execution in 1982. Today it is the main method used in the United States.

Life on Death Row

- As of July 2016 there were 2,905 people on death row in the United States.
- In 2013, 56 percent of death row prisoners were white, while 42 percent were black.
- The Bureau of Justice Statistics reports that the average time between sentencing and execution is longer than sixteen years.

American Opinions of the Death Penalty

- According to a 2016 Gallup poll, 50 percent of Americans believe the death penalty is applied fairly; 44 percent believe it is not applied fairly.
- Gallup polling over the years has shown that the lowest level of support for the death penalty was in 1972, when just 57 percent of Americans favored the death penalty. The highest level of support occurred in 1994, when 80 percent of Americans supported the death penalty. As of 2016, 60 percent of Americans said they favored the death penalty, down from 66 percent who supported it in 2010.
- A different 2016 poll—this one taken by the Pew Research Center—found that only about half of all Americans (49 percent) favored the death penalty for people convicted of murder; 42 percent opposed it.
- The Pew Research Center also found that more Republicans (72 percent) than Democrats (34 percent) favor the death penalty.

Related Organizations and Websites

American Enterprise Institute
1789 Massachusetts Ave. NW
Washington, DC 20036
website: www.aei.org

The American Enterprise Institute is a public policy think tank dedicated to defending human dignity, expanding human potential, and building a freer and safer world. It produces research, articles, and other commentary on a variety of issues, including the death penalty.

Campaign to End the Death Penalty
PO Box 25730
Chicago, IL 60625
website: nodeathpenalty.org

This national grassroots organization is dedicated to ending capital punishment. It has chapters across the United States.

Death Penalty Information Center
1015 Eighteenth St. NW, Suite 704
Washington, DC 20036
website: www.deathpenaltyinfo.org

The Death Penalty Information Center is a nonprofit organization that educates the public about capital punishment issues. The center releases an annual report featuring the latest statistics on the death penalty.

Gallup

The Gallup Building
901 F St. NW
Washington, DC 20004
website: www.gallup.com

Gallup is an organization that conducts polls on a variety of topics, including the death penalty.

The Heritage Foundation

214 Massachusetts Ave NE
Washington, DC 20002-4999
website: www.heritage.org

The Heritage Foundation is a conservative think tank that publishes research on various research and articles on domestic, economic, foreign and defense policy. Several articles in support of the death penalty can be found on its website.

The Innocence Project

40 Worth St., Suite 701
New York, NY 10013
website: www.innocenceproject.org

Lawyers Peter Neufeld and Barry Scheck founded the Innocence Project in 1992. Using DNA evidence, the group works to exonerate people who are wrongly accused.

Justice for All

website: www.jfa.net

Justice for All is an organization headquartered in Houston, Texas, that promotes criminal justice reform and defends use of the death penalty. It provides advocacy information for the victims of violent crimes.

Murder Victims' Families for Reconciliation (MVFR)
5800 Faringdon Place
Raleigh, NC 27609
website: www.mvfr.org

MVFR is made up of family members of murder victims and the executed. Together they advocate for ending the death penalty.

National Coalition to Abolish the Death Penalty
1620 L St. NW, Suite 250
Washington, DC 20036
website: www.ncadp.org

As its name suggests, the National Coalition to Abolish the Death Penalty works to end the practice of capital punishment in the United States and abroad. The organization believes it is better to address the causes of violence than to punish violent criminals with death.

Pew Research Center
1615 L St. NW, Suite 800
Washington, DC 20036
website: www.pewresearch.org

The Pew Research Center is a nonpartisan group that conducts public opinion polls and other research on a variety of issues, including the death penalty.

For Further Research

Books

Jenny Cromie and Lynn M. Zott, eds., *The Death Penalty*. Farmington Hills, MI: Greenhaven, 2013.

D.J. Herda, *The Death Penalty:* Furman v. Georgia. New York: Enslow, 2017.

Mario Marazziti, *13 Ways of Looking at the Death Penalty*. New York: Seven Stories, 2015.

Noel Merino, ed., *Death Penalty*. Farmington Hills, MI: Greenhaven, 2015.

Carla Mooney, *Is the Death Penalty Just?* San Diego: ReferencePoint, 2014.

Nancy Mullane, *Life After Murder: Five Men in Search of Redemption*. New York: PublicAffairs, 2012.

Nanon M. Williams, *The Darkest Hour: Stories and Interviews from Death Row*. Dallas: Goodmedia, 2012.

Periodicals

Frank R. Baumgartner and Anna W. Dietrich, "Most Death Penalty Sentences Are Overturned. Here's Why That Matters," *Washington Post*, March 17, 2015.

Emily Bazelon, "Where the Death Penalty Still Lives," *New York Times*, August 23, 2016.

John Donohue, "Does the Death Penalty Deter Killers?," *Newsweek*, August 19, 2015.

Max Ehrenfreund, "There's Still No Evidence That Executions Deter Criminals," *Washington Post*, April 30, 2014.

Charles Lane, "The Death Penalty and Racism," *American Interest*, November 1, 2010.

Michael A. Ramos, "Don't Abolish the Death Penalty, Make the System Work," *San Bernardino (CA) Sun*, October 23, 2016.

Jeffrey Toobin, "The Strange Case of the American Death Penalty," *New Yorker*, December 21, 2016.

David Von Drehle, "The Death of the Death Penalty: Why the Era of Capital Punishment Is Ending," *Time*, June 8, 2015.

Internet Sources

Amnesty International, "Death Penalty." www.amnesty.org/en/what-we -do/death-penalty.

Clark County Prosecuting Attorney, "The Death Penalty." www.clark prosecutor.org/html/death/death.htm.

CNN Library, "Death Penalty Fast Facts," CNN.com, January 29, 2017. www.cnn.com/2013/07/19/us/death-penalty-fast-facts.

"Death Penalty: An Overview," Cornell University Law School, Legal Information Institute. www.law.cornell.edu/wex/death_penalty.

Jeffrey A. Fagan, "Capital Punishment: Deterrent Effects & Capital Costs," Columbia Law School. http://facade1.law.columbia.edu/law _school/communications/reports/summer06/capitalpunish.

Index

Note: Boldface page numbers indicate illustrations.

African Americans
  death penalty is disproportionately
    applied to, 35–37
  as percentage of total death row
    population, 31
aggravating circumstance, 12, 30, 31
Allen, Howard, 55
Alvord, Gary, 57
American Civil Liberties Union
  (ACLU), 46
American Enterprise Institute, 71
American Society for the Abolition of
  Capital Punishment, 10
Associated Press, 56
Atkinson, Lee, 28

Ban Ki-moon, 13
Barton, Corey Robert, 19, 55
Bellivier, Florence, 25
Berns, Nancy, 60
Bible, 9, 45, 50
Blecker, Robert, 41, 44–45, 57–58
Bloodsworth, Kirk, 38
Boston Marathon bombing (2015),
  54, 62
Brennan, William J., 48
Bright, Stephen B., 34
Brown, Jeannie, 45
Brown, Richard, 45
Bureau of Justice Statistics, US, 30,
  56, 57, 70
Bureau of Prisons, US, 56–57

California, voter support for death

penalty in, **17**
Campaign to End the Death Penalty,
  71
Charleston (SC) church shooting
  (2015), 8–9, 60–61
Christopoulos, Dimitris, 25
Cloninger, Dale, 16
closure
  death penalty provides, 53–54
  is an illusion, 60
Code of Hammurabi, 9
Coke, Tanya, 60–61, 62, 63
convicted murderers
  cannot be rehabilitated, 20
  costs to incarcerate, 56–57
  execution should cause suffering for,
    43–45
  families of, 63
  many can be rehabilitated, 64
  who served sentence and killed
    again, **55**
  See also death row inmates
crimes of passion, death penalty does
  not deter, 25

death penalty
  calls to abolish, 10–11, 12–13
  confirms value of life, 42–43
  as deterrence against crime
    argument against, 21–26
    argument for, 15–20
    debate over, 14
  as ethical
    argument against, 46–51
    argument for, 41–45
    debate over, 40
  as fairly imposed

About the Author

Stephanie Watson is a freelance writer based in Providence, Rhode Island. For nearly two decades, she has covered the latest health and science research for publications such as WebMD, Healthline, and Harvard Medical School. Watson has also authored more than two dozen books for young adults, including *The Future of Technology: What Is the Future of Self-Driving Cars?* and *Forgotten Youth: Incarcerated Youth*.